Use Your Palabras, Jovita!

How This Brave Journalist Stood for Justice

Written by
Keishia
Lee Louis

Illustrated by
Diego Alejandro
Escobar Triana

"To my English Language Learning and Journalism students in GCPS. You have inspired me in more ways than you know!"--k.l.l.

"To Gloria, for opening my eyes" --d.a.e.t.

Use Your Palabras, Jovita!
Copyright © 2025 by Keishia Lee Louis
Illustration Copyright © 2025 Free Sparrows Press
All rights reserved. No part of this book may be reproduced or transmitted in any form or by any means without the written permission of the author or publisher.

Publisher: Free Sparrows Kids, an imprint of RelaSonship, LLC
Dacula, GA 30019

Hardcover ISBN: 978-1-966011-04-0
Paperback ISBN: 978-1-966011-05-7
Library of Congress Control Number: 2025912825

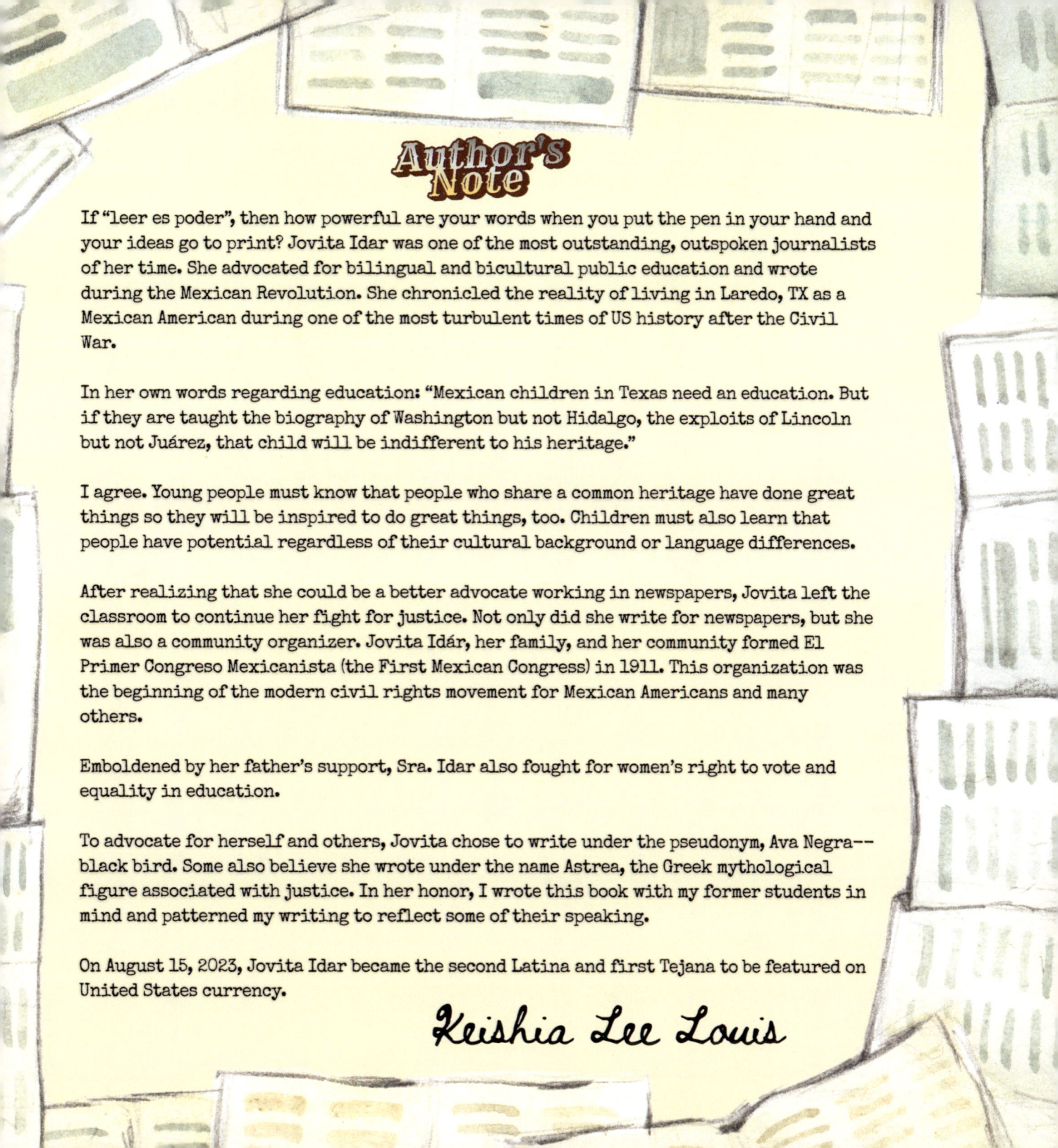

Author's Note

If "leer es poder", then how powerful are your words when you put the pen in your hand and your ideas go to print? Jovita Idar was one of the most outstanding, outspoken journalists of her time. She advocated for bilingual and bicultural public education and wrote during the Mexican Revolution. She chronicled the reality of living in Laredo, TX as a Mexican American during one of the most turbulent times of US history after the Civil War.

In her own words regarding education: "Mexican children in Texas need an education. But if they are taught the biography of Washington but not Hidalgo, the exploits of Lincoln but not Juárez, that child will be indifferent to his heritage."

I agree. Young people must know that people who share a common heritage have done great things so they will be inspired to do great things, too. Children must also learn that people have potential regardless of their cultural background or language differences.

After realizing that she could be a better advocate working in newspapers, Jovita left the classroom to continue her fight for justice. Not only did she write for newspapers, but she was also a community organizer. Jovita Idár, her family, and her community formed El Primer Congreso Mexicanista (the First Mexican Congress) in 1911. This organization was the beginning of the modern civil rights movement for Mexican Americans and many others.

Emboldened by her father's support, Sra. Idar also fought for women's right to vote and equality in education.

To advocate for herself and others, Jovita chose to write under the pseudonym, Ava Negra-- black bird. Some also believe she wrote under the name Astrea, the Greek mythological figure associated with justice. In her honor, I wrote this book with my former students in mind and patterned my writing to reflect some of their speaking.

On August 15, 2023, Jovita Idar became the second Latina and first Tejana to be featured on United States currency.

Keishia Lee Louis

Use your palabras Jovita!
The words rang out like bells through the halls of our hogar.
Mi padre believed that all of his children, boys and girls
niños y niñas,

Spoken... or written to defend and define the beauty of our culture.

Las palabras – escriben sobre las injusticias.
Yes! Write about why we are people
who should be treated fairly!

I write about why we should learn in Spanish and in English in our schools.

Our words bring la luz

shining like

las estrellas

piercing the darkness of the night sky.

Papa said, "You are smart, *inteligente* Jovita! You are strong. Be brave enough to express yourself not just for you, or our *familia,* but for all the people you love.

Especially when they cannot speak--or write--for themselves.

He urged me to write for La Crónica. I did.
Las palabras YOUR words, have power.
More power than fists, more power than guns.

"Words are what they will remember for generations," he said.

"Our mother tongue should be honored in all her beauty, Like a *mariposa*, a beautiful butterfly with delicate wings, las palabras bring hope.

I write about why we must have peaceful borders free from the Rangers' brutal treatment.

Woodrow Wilson, el presidente must hear us. Our palabras, written in newspapers, make their way to the White House long before telephones or television.

But President Wilson was not the only one who heard us...

The governor sent the Texas Rangers. They brought guns. They brought hammers and axes to destroy our press—El Progreso—when our words got too fuerte, sharp. Like a hacha!

We, mi gente, mis antepasados, had not moved. The lines had moved around us. Like a lasso, we were looped into a new way of living.

Mis estudiantes were not being treated fairly. They did not have the good libros other niños had. They did not have the good desks, playgrounds, and libraries. But their parents paid taxes like everyone else.

They would not destroy the press.
Our newspaper would stand.
Our voices would be heard.
Didn't the president believe that idea for us?

Por mis estudiantes?
Por mi familia?

One day, when I was away...

No! La Crónica still stood! I would work with them again!

And if they took La Cronica, Evolucion would rise!

Mis palabras have power!

Words to Know

palabras	words
hogar	home
mi padre	my father
niños y niñas	boys and girls
todos ocho de nosotros	all eight of us
escriben sobre las injusticias	write of the injustices
la luz	the light
las estrellas	the stars
inteligente	intelligent
familia	family
mariposa	butterfly
el presidente	the president
fuerte	sharp
hacha	axe, hatchet; also a brilliant person
mi gente	my people; my folks
mis antepasados	my ancestors
mis estudiantes	my students
libros	books
comida	food
mi corazon	my heart
silencio	silence

Resources

1) Grant, T., Charboneau, Y. (2024, December 16). Jovita Idár. Encyclopedia Britannica. https://www.britannica.com/biography/Jovita-Idar

2) Smithsonian American Women's History Museum. (n.d.). ¡Que viva Jovita!: Celebrating journalist and activist Jovita Idar. Smithsonian Institution. https://womenshistory.si.edu/blog/que-viva-jovita-celebrating-journalist-and-activist-jovita-idar

3) PBS NewsHour. (2021, March 31). Jovita Idar's fight for the rights of women and Mexican immigrants. PBS. https://www.pbs.org/newshour/show/jovita-idars-fight-for-the-rights-of-women-and-mexican-immigrant

www.ingramcontent.com/pod-product-compliance
Lightning Source LLC
Chambersburg PA
CBRC091208010526
44107CB00022B/1260